Driftwood

Driftwood

Poems by

Henry Wolstat

Cover design by Shay Culligan
Cover photo by Henk Nugter

ISBN: 978-1-63980-141-1

Kelsay Books
502 South 1040 East, A-119
American Fork, Utah 84003
Kelsaybooks.com

Dedication
for my wife and editor, Marj Radin
who kept me going

Acknowledgments

Thanks to the publications in which versions of these poems have appeared:

Baseball Bard: "October's Heroes," "Jackie," "Big Papi"

Haikuniverse: "Bix," "Muddy River"

Muddy River Poetry Review: "The Last Leaf"

Scissortail Quarterly #4: "Siesta Beach"

Soul Lit: "Andalusia," "Play Me"

Sweetycat Press: Around the World Landscapes & Cityscapes: "Cycling in Holland;" Stories & Poems in the Song of Life: "Lady Day and Prez;" Beautiful In the Eye of the Beholder: "I'll Follow You;" Movement Our Bodies in Motion: "Speedy as a Turtle"

Verse-Virtual Poems and Articles: "A Well-Mixed Martini," "A Sunny Warm Day"

Contents

Landscapes

Driftwood

Like driftwood
I sometimes feel
I've been cast
into the oceans
of life, depending
on the tides
to carry me
to all the
destinations I've
reached for
a short visit
or a long stay.

Pura Vida

Flying past a volcano
Smoke billowing
From its deep crater
Costa Rica fading
Rain forests
Enveloped in verdant
Mists, flora and fauna
A presence felt
Seen and heard.
I glory in the
Essence of your
Soul.
A brief encounter
With your
Pura Vida.

Cycling in Holland

Windmills and tulips
Windmills and tulips

Cycling along the canals
in the land of orange,
coronation day,
Beatrix to Wilhelm,
a sea of orange
celebrated from
dawn to midnight,

Amsterdam, Gouda,
Leiden, Haarlem,
fields of flowers,
a blanket of hues

Windmills and tulips
Windmills and tulips

Short Vacation

Long drive
Garden State Parkway
Ocean City
boardwalk
midway rides
ferris wheel
ice cream
donuts, fried
everything
friendly strangers
loving family
scene from
the 1950's?
you can go
home again.

A Sunny Warm Day

There's an alligator
in my front yard
lounging in a pond
enjoying the sun
while we sit
on the porch
sipping a cool drink.
It's been two
years since
we traveled
to our favorite
southern destination
joining all the
snowbirds basking
contentedly like
a purring reptile.

Crystal Beach

Crystal Beach,
not much of a beach,
on the shores
of Lake Erie,
a stone's throw
from old Buffalo
and American girls.

Hitching from
our Toronto homes
with our adolescent
hormones raging,
fortifying our resolve
with unbelievable donuts,
our sole diet for
several days of
total freedom.

Those days are
long gone but
I can still taste
those sweet treats,
our drugs of choice.

Siesta Beach

The early morning hordes
Low tide beckoning
Walking the hard sand
Birds hovering the
Quiet surf, the baking
Sun drenched sky
A lonely parasail.
Soon the parade
Of daily beach
Goers pulling their
Wagons, chairs
Poised like military
Armaments.
The walkers empty
Out to their daily
Activities as the
Beach people fill
The hours worshipping
The sun and the sea.
Another day in
Paradise.

Yosemite

El Capitan, Bridal Veil Falls, Mirror Lake,
Ansel Adams captured your majestic beauty.
I've hiked your long trails,
Cycled through the valley,
Ice skated in Curry Village.

Almost fifty years ago
We camped besides a rock,
Awoke to an avid group of
Rock climbers surrounding
Us and our almost born daughter.

When I last returned
Your magic had not lessened,
A luxury hotel, not a tent,
With a view of Yosemite Falls
By moonlight
Framed my visit,
But the memory of that
First time in that glorious
Park remains indelible.

Andalusia

Andalusia, I glide past your
Sparkling olive tree groves
On a mountain path surrounded
By white-washed villages,
Castle ruins and nature parks.
Seville, Cordoba, Granada,
Magical cities where
Maimonides, Halevi, Gabirol
Resided centuries ago.
Cordoba, the Jewish quarter
Where there are no Jews.
The old synagogue,
The Maimonides statue,
Give evidence of a lost culture,
An exiled people.
Granada, the Alhambra,
Its Moorish beauty,
Modified by the crusading
Conquerors.
Where Isabel sent Columbus
On his journey financed
By Jews she soon expelled.
Conversion or expulsion
Were the choices.
St. Teresa of Avila,
Partly Jewish was
Subject to the inquisition.
She, who added to the beauty,
Of the massive cathedral
Within Alhambra's walls.

I stood in awe of Andalusia's
Treasures and whispered
"I'm back".
Sunset at the Miramar,
A silent "Sh'ma"

Running

My Favorite Run

My Favorite run,
four miles over
two bridges spanning
the Charles River.

The blue waters
carry me along,
the paths warmed
by the morning sun.

Feeling ageless
at a turtle's pace,
my body moves
steadily from
start to finish.

Fatigue is often
my reward
for my effort.

Olympian's give
their all to
finish a race,
my race
is not finished.

Speedy As a Turtle

Muddy River,
I run along
your tree lined
path,
my pace slow,
my age advanced.

Once I was
Hermès with
winged feet,
floating with
a runner's high.

Mile after mile,
marathon after marathon.

A turtle at
the river bank
sidles toward
the path.

Entranced, I follow
it's steady course.
Speed is no longer
of importance.

Our measured pace
propelling us
to our mutual
goals.

Independence Day 5K

On Independence Day
I ran 3.1 miles,
the first road race
in over a long year of
daily walking, running,
masking, and social isolation

Old friends were there,
looking much older,
but still able to move
one foot after another.

My love walked beside
me for moral support
and handing me
water as needed,

It felt like a miraculous
re-emergence into normality.
I finished the race dead
last, but with a smile
on my face and a
renewed appreciation
for life.

Morning is My Mistress

Rising in the early morning
I greet the sunrise with
all my senses
like a long lost lover.
out for a run or a walk
surrounded by silence;
my world awakens.

Out For a Run

This morning like
most mornings for
the last half century,
I put on my sneakers
and headed out for a run.
The leaves were turning,
the sun was shining,
how great to be alive.

My pace has slowed
over the years
and little old ladies
with walkers now
easily pass me.

But, like the tortoise
and the hare,
I'll get to the
finish line
at my own speed.

Each blade of grass,
each ancient tree,
a witness to my
longevity and
running memories.
How great to be alive!

Running in the Time of Covid-19

Cancellations, postponements
not a race to be found
the runner laments.
wasted miles, tough training,
no longer a possible PR
or even a struggling finish,
gone are the Boston hordes.

But joy still abounds
the loneliness of the long distance
runner no longer signifies sadness.

Social distancing now the norm
as we walk or run these quiet
streets and roads welcoming
the early signs of Spring,
the sprouting of magnolia and
dogwood trees, daffodils and crocuses.

Soon enough the racers and pacers
will fill these empty spaces
and our racing aspirations
will be born anew.

A Winter Run

The joys of winter, cold and white,
No longer appeal to my aging soul.
I seek the warmth of southern climes,
T-shirted and shorted
As the palm trees
Sway on my path.
Each step invigorates
My almost youthful stride.
Seeking the sun
Makes each run
A gift of love
And a new
Joy of winter.

Rage over a Missed Run

I missed my run
My body is sore
It cannot be done

It's no longer fun
Life is such a bore
Without a daily run.

Lying here in the sun
Who could ask for more?
No run have I done.

But I move not one
Step from my door
I just cannot run.

I'll soon weigh a ton
Just sleep and snore
My life will be done.

These happy years gone
What else lies in store?
I missed my run
It just cannot be done.

Aging?

On a crisp December day
many men in their
late eighties are
content to sit by
a fire, wrapped in
warm, lounging apparel,
streaming Netflix
on their smart devises,
a refreshing toddy
in their hands.

Others prefer
to imbibe the
cold winter air
of an energetic, but
slow run along
a river path
wrapped in the
rays of a
bright sun.

#BraveLikeGabe

Running can be a lonely sport.
You only have yourself
As you traverse the roads,
The trails, or the track.

At the finish line
You may have come in
First, last, or somewhere
In between.

But you finished
With or without pain,
With or without that
Joyful feeling of accomplishment.

Gabe was an inspiration
With only limited days
In her life
She ran to the end.

Some die with their boots on.
She died with her sneakers on.
Long live those who follow
In her footsteps.

Aging and Other Considerations

Play Me

Hey fool, play me.
Let my shiny, brassy,
Curvaceous body
Seduce you.
Play me and
Soar to the sky
In the spirit of
Trane, Bird,
And the Prez.
Press your lips
Around my mouth.
Blow a devil may
Care riff,
And let your
Fingers walk
Up and down
My silky keys.
Wail and sing,
Scream and shout.
Play me with
All your might
Before you lay me
In that velvet bed.

Lady Day and Prez

Sitting at the bar
Of the Towne Tavern,
Once Toronto's finest jazz bar,
Sipping my one beer.
Knowing even then,
In my twenty-third year,
I was witness to a
Never forgotten gig.
Lady Day, how every note
You sang rang out
With the blues and
The rhythm of your
Battered and celebrated life.
And you, Prez, in your
Pork pie hat blew
Sounds that resonated
In my memory years later.
You both were wasted,
Facing death within a year.
But you're both very
Much alive in my soul.

October's Heroes

Another series creeps
To its inevitable end.
The boys of summer
Accompany the falling leaves.
We sat on folding chairs
In the home of a more affluent relative
And watched the games
In black and white on a
Miniscule TV set
When it was truly
The national pastime.
DiMaggio, Feller,
Aaron, Robinson.
Magical names we
All knew and admired.
What's the hurry?
Tinkers to Evers to Chance,
A balletic pas de trois.
A stolen base,
A well placed bunt.
I remember those days.

Jackie

Post WW11 and
a new day for
"organized" baseball
a young black
Negro League all star
was signed by
the Brooklyn Dodgers,
but first, a stint
with the AAA
Montreal Royals.
I was twelve
years old and
selling refreshments
at the old stadium
of the Toronto
Maple Leaf team.
All eyes were
on the field
when the Royals
came to town.
Jackie was the
focus of our
attention.
I can't remember
who won or lost
but baseball
had changed.

Big Papi

Big Papi
You're the man.
When the Sox
needed a hit
you delivered.
When the city
needed a boost
after the
marathon bombing
you inspired
Boston Strong.
Now, you're
enshrined in Cooperstown.
A perfect fit!

A Fantasy

In Greek mythology
a centaur is a symbol
of masculine power with a
weakness for wine, women
and violent behavior.

If I were a centaur
I would trot through
the woods, enjoying
the flora and wishing
that a beautiful woman
would pass by bearing
a carafe of red wine
and sharing a picnic
on the grass near
a babbling brook.

And then riding
on my equine back
towards a spectacular
and glorious sunset.

Then I would awake
from this reverie
and realize how
sexist this wishful
fantasy really was.

I'll Follow You

I've never seen
the Northern Lights
of an Icelandic night,
nor a raging bull
in Pamplona.
O'er the steppes
of Central Asia
I've never set
my wandering feet.
But I've seen
the beauty of
your smile,
the love in
your eyes,
felt the warmth
of your arms,
and anywhere
you roam,
I'll follow your
footsteps to the
ends of the earth.

As If

As if life
gave me choices
and I always
picked the
right one.

As if love
was easy
and my heart
knew the
right direction.

As if my
words were
always truthful
and never
painful.

As if happiness
was around
the corner,
I would have
no regrets.

Letter to My 75 Year Old Self

Twelve years ago
you ran your last
marathon in Boston.
Your wife and son
produced a chap book
of your writings,
your family and friends
celebrated your birthday
in person, not virtually.

Little did you know
that twelve years later
your birthday wishes
would be streamed
and Zoomed on
a small screen,
though you're now
fully vaccinated
against a plague
you could not
have predicted.

I don't know how
much time you
have left, but
I'm so pleased
that you continued
to live each day
like it was your
last.

A Life

I went to a funeral
today of a dear
soul whose life
spanned the century
between two pandemics,
between countless wars
and many technological
and scientific advances.

She was eulogized
by her family
as one who had
lived a simple
but rewarding life.

How do we look
at someone whose
years seem unimportant
in the greater picture
of world events,
yet so meaningful
to those who have
been touched by her?

A Chance Encounter With A Stranger

Home is where
the heart is.
No more moving
and seeking
greener pastures.
Yet, when I
encounter someone
wearing a ball cap
or T-shirt with
the name of
my hometown,
I stop them,
engage them
in conversation,
shedding my shyness.
I suppose that
eternal search
for home never
ends for
some of us.

A Whisper

A whisper so low
That the words dissolve
As soon as they are
Spoken.
A song that lingers
In the mind of a
Beloved.
A touch that is barely
Felt on silken
Skin.
Memories so fleeting
Of one's long
Life.
A brief moment,
But recalled and
Treasured.

The Last Leaf

Stark blue sky,
tree outside my window,
one solitary leaf
hanging from its branches,
the frost covered ground.

Only last spring
it was hopeful,
buds waiting to blossom
to a vibrant green.

Came fall, the green
turned to hues of yellow
and orange sparkling
like gems, the sun
beaming on the leaves.

The days grew shorter,
colder, the foliage now
brown and falling until
one lonely leaf remained.

I hold on like that leaf
in the autumn of my life,
my contemporaries falling
as withered leaves.

In time, I too, will
wither and move on,
but for now,
I will greet the sun
and moon each day
and remain hopeful
for the next generation.

Lost Lives

My mother had
a twin brother.
She never talked
about him
except to say
that he moved
to the big city
and was never
heard from again
and just vanished
like the millions
of Jews, victims
of the Holocaust.

She also had
a younger sister
who she mourned,
regretting she
never brought
her to Canada,
unlike one other
sister she paid
passage for.

How I wish
I had known them.

A Well-Mixed Martini

I've always enjoyed a well-mixed martini,
The gin and the vermouth in
Proper proportions,
Garnished with olives and a twist
Of lemon or lime.
I'm reminded of Nick and Nora Charles
And their 'Thin Man' adventures,
So elegantly filmed.
My own level of sophistication
Doesn't equal
That era of the late thirties
When high hats and Bugattis
Hardly anticipated a century
Of destruction and chaos.

HAIKUS

when Bix blew his horn
flappers danced from dusk to dawn
ah! bathtub gin!

muddy river
your banks are wide
loons can hide

I'm aging quickly
my years are checked off and gone
music is my balm.

early morning run
I greet the rising sun
coffee my fuel

baying at the moon
old dogs learn no new tricks
time for a nap.

summer came early
flora flourishing in June
wilting on my run

each minute of life
blows by like a flash of light,
yes, a martini!

on rainy spring days
I turn into a flaneur
treading my life's roads

wild turkeys cross roads
their offspring follow in rows
drivers screech and stop!

sunrise fills my senses
a tender embrace and I
move wind at my back.

pink flamingos in Boston?
harbingers of spring
don't fly away.

we 80 year olds
have gone wild
vacced and relaxed.

About the Author

Henry Wolstat, a retired psychiatrist in his late 80s, was born in Toronto, Canada and now lives in Brookline, Massachusetts with his wife. He is passionate about poetry, music, and running.

His poems have been published in *Baseball Bard, Haikuniverse, Muddy River Poetry Review, Scissortail Quarterly, Soul-Lit,* and *Sweetycat Press, Verse-Virtual Poems* and *Articles.*

Made in the USA
Coppell, TX
30 June 2022

79420956R00038